T0403048

Too Cute!

Baby Sheep

by Betsy Rathburn

BLASTOFF!
Beginners

BELLWETHER MEDIA
MINNEAPOLIS, MN

Blastoff! Beginners are developed by literacy experts and educators to meet the needs of early readers. These engaging informational texts support young children as they begin reading about their world. Through simple language and high frequency words paired with crisp, colorful photos, Blastoff! Beginners launch young readers into the universe of independent reading.

Blastoff! Universe

Reading Level — Grade K — Blastoff! Beginners
Grades 1-3 — Blastoff! Readers
Grade 4 — Blastoff! Discovery

Sight Words in This Book 🔍

and	eat	may	this
are	have	play	to
at	in	the	
big	jump	their	
each	look	they	

This edition first published in 2024 by Bellwether Media, Inc.

No part of this publication may be reproduced in whole or in part without written permission of the publisher. For information regarding permission, write to Bellwether Media, Inc., Attention: Permissions Department, 6012 Blue Circle Drive, Minnetonka, MN 55343.

Library of Congress Cataloging-in-Publication Data

Names: Rathburn, Betsy, author.
Title: Baby sheep / by Betsy Rathburn.
Description: Minneapolis, MN : Bellwether Media, Inc., 2024. | Series: Blastoff! Beginners. Too cute! | Includes bibliographical references and index. | Audience: Ages 4-7 | Audience: Grades K-1
Identifiers: LCCN 2023000128 (print) | LCCN 2023000129 (ebook) | ISBN 9798886874068 (library binding) | ISBN 9798886875942 (ebook)
Subjects: LCSH: Lambs--Juvenile literature.
Classification: LCC SF376.5 .R38 2024 (print) | LCC SF376.5 (ebook) | DDC 636.3/07--dc23/eng/20230112
LC record available at https://lccn.loc.gov/2023000128
LC ebook record available at https://lccn.loc.gov/2023000129

Editor: Rachael Barnes   Designer: Laura Sowers

Printed in the United States of America, North Mankato, MN.

Table of Contents

A Baby Sheep!

Look at the baby sheep. Hello, lamb!

Farm Life

Most lambs are born in barns. They may have **siblings**.

barn

siblings

Lambs are small.
They have
soft **wool**.

wool

They **bleat**.
They are loud!

bleating

11

They drink
mom's milk.
They eat grass
and hay.

mom

They jump and
play outside.
They kick
and butt heads!

jumping

Lambs are close
to their group.
They stick
together!

Growing Up!

They grow bigger.
Their wool
grows thick.

Farmers cut their wool each spring. This **yearling** stays cool!

yearling

farmer

21

Baby Sheep Facts

Sheep Life Stages

lamb   yearling   adult

A Day in the Life

drink
mom's
milk

eat hay   play

Glossary

bleat

to make a loud crying sound

siblings

brothers and sisters

wool

the soft, thick hair of sheep

yearling

a sheep that is between one and two years old

To Learn More

ON THE WEB

FACTSURFER

Factsurfer.com gives you a safe, fun way to find more information.

1. Go to www.factsurfer.com.

2. Enter "baby sheep" into the search box and click 🔍.

3. Select your book cover to see a list of related content.

Index

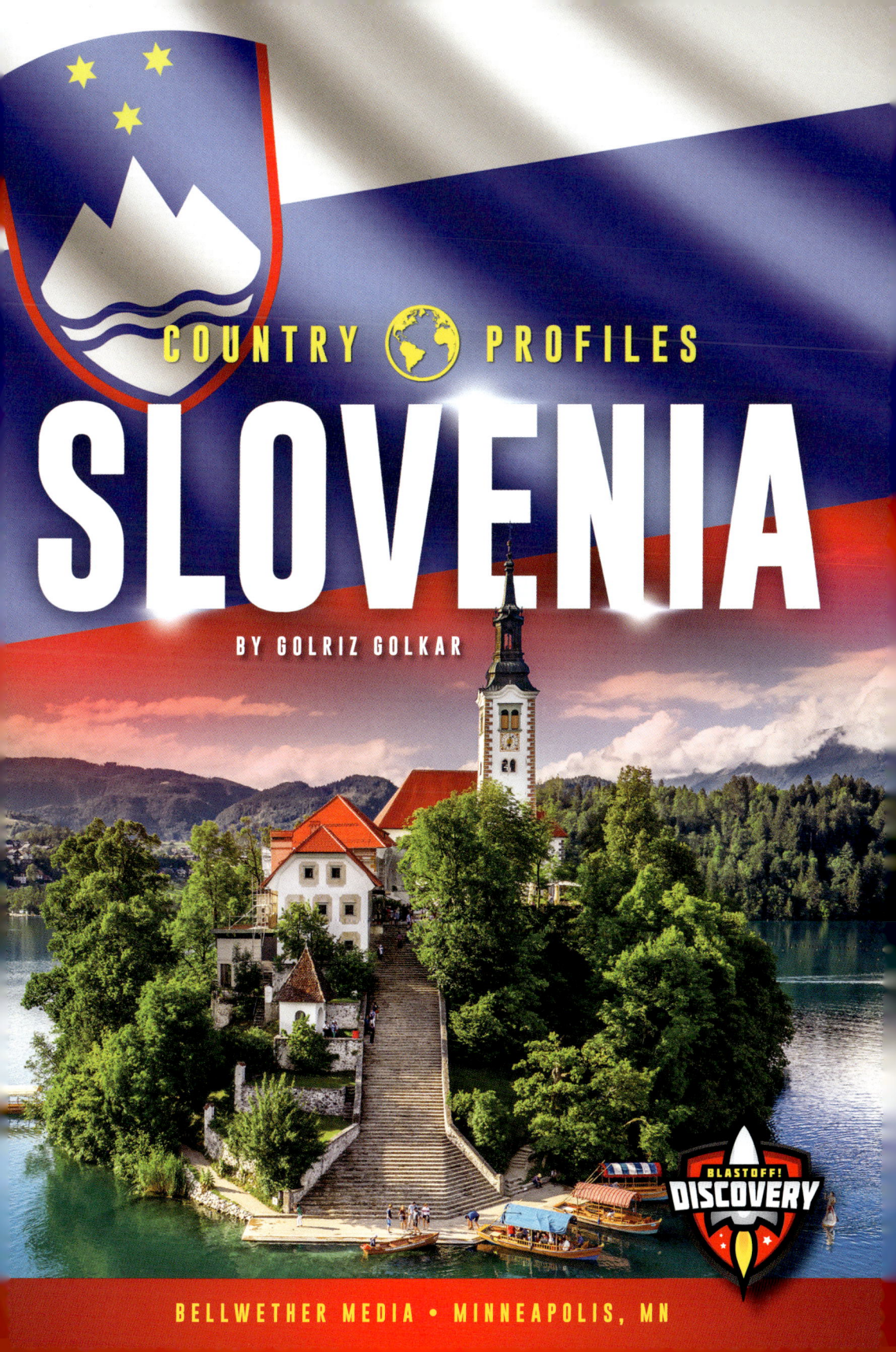

BY GOLRIZ GOLKAR

COUNTRY PROFILES

SLOVENIA

BELLWETHER MEDIA • MINNEAPOLIS, MN

Blastoff! Discovery launches a new mission: reading to learn. Filled with facts and features, each book offers you an exciting new world to explore!

BLASTOFF! UNIVERSE

GRADE K

GRADES 1-3

GRADE 4

This edition first published in 2023 by Bellwether Media, Inc.

No part of this publication may be reproduced in whole or in part without written permission of the publisher.
For information regarding permission, write to Bellwether Media, Inc., Attention: Permissions Department,
6012 Blue Circle Drive, Minnetonka, MN 55343.

Library of Congress Cataloging-in-Publication Data

Names: Golkar, Golriz, author.
Title: Slovenia / Golriz Golkar.
Description: Minneapolis, MN : Bellwether Media, Inc., 2023. | Series: Blastoff! Discovery. Country profiles | Includes bibliographical references and index. | Audience: Ages 7-13 | Audience: Grades 4-6 | Summary: "Engaging images accompany information about Slovenia. The combination of high-interest subject matter and narrative text is intended for students in grades 3 through 8"– Provided by publisher.
Identifiers: LCCN 2022050038 (print) | LCCN 2022050039 (ebook) | ISBN 9798886871487 (library binding) | ISBN 9798886872743 (ebook)
Subjects: LCSH: Slovenia–Juvenile literature.
Classification: LCC DR1360 .G655 2023 (print) | LCC DR1360 (ebook) | DDC 949.73–dc23/eng/20221018
LC record available at https://lccn.loc.gov/2022050038
LC ebook record available at https://lccn.loc.gov/2022050039

Editor: Rachael Barnes   Designer: Brittany McIntosh

Printed in the United States of America, North Mankato, MN.

TABLE OF CONTENTS

CITY OF DRAGONS

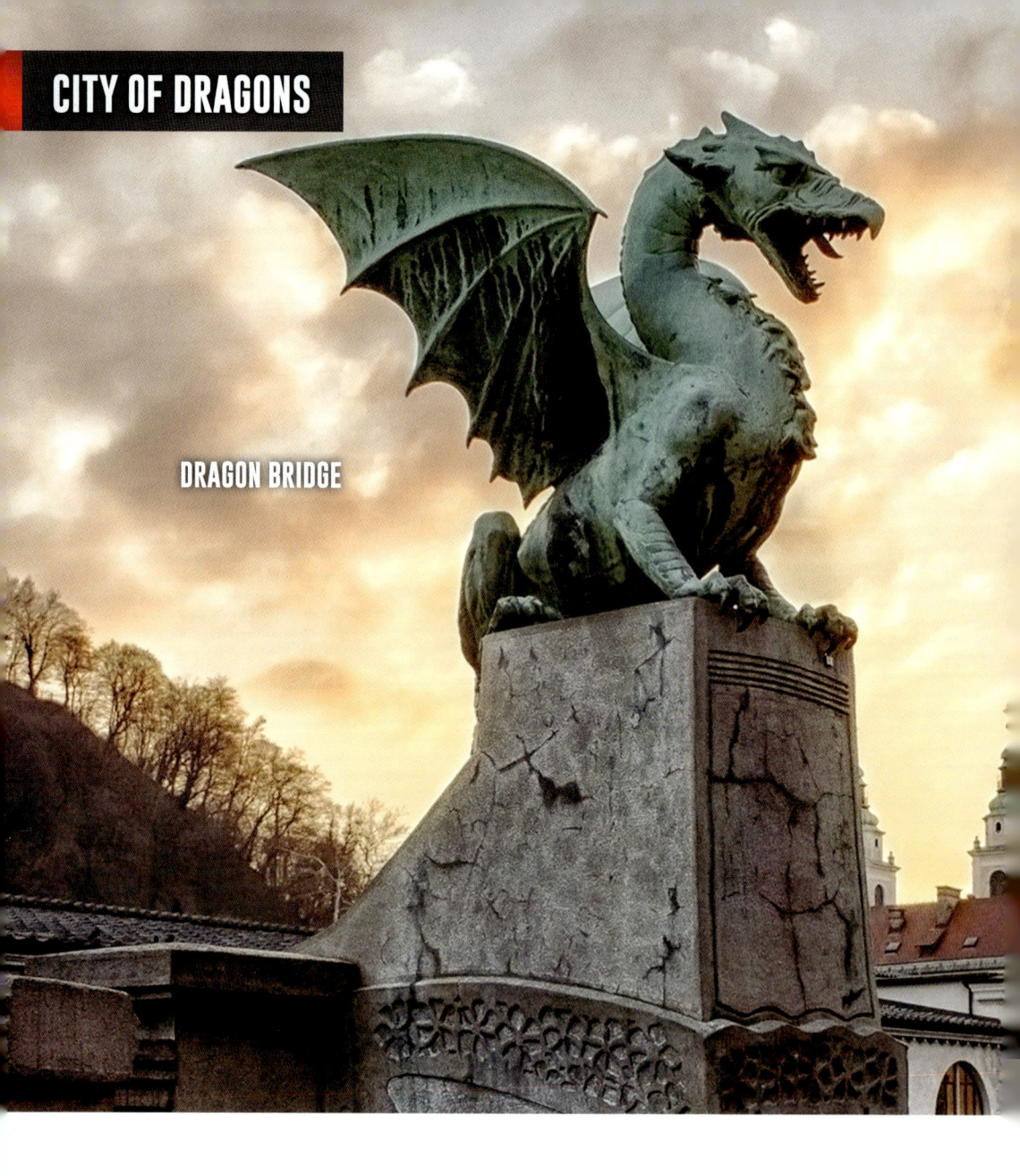

DRAGON BRIDGE

A family climbs the Ljubljana Castle tower. They take in a beautiful city view. After walking the castle grounds, they ride the **funicular** back into the city. The family strolls across Dragon Bridge. They take a picture next to one of the city's dragon sculptures.

OTHER TOP SITES

PREDJAMA CASTLE

ŠKOCJAN CAVES

TRIGLAV NATIONAL PARK

TRIPLE BRIDGE

THE DRAGON PROTECTOR

A Slovene legend says a hero in Greek mythology fought off a dragon in Ljubljana. Over time, the dragon became a city symbol. It protects Ljubljana and represents wisdom, courage, and power.

For lunch, they walk to a restaurant near the popular Prešeren Square. They enjoy *bograč* stew made with meat and potatoes. Then they visit the National Gallery. They admire the paintings of famous Slovene artists. **Architecture**, delicious **cuisine**, and art offer just a taste of Slovenia's rich **culture**!

5

A FORMER REPUBLIC

Slovenia used to be a republic of the former country of Yugoslavia. In 1991, the six republics of Yugoslavia became independent countries.

AUSTRIA

MARIBOR

ITALY

LJUBLJANA

CELJE

SLOVENIA

KOPER

ADRIATIC SEA

CROATIA

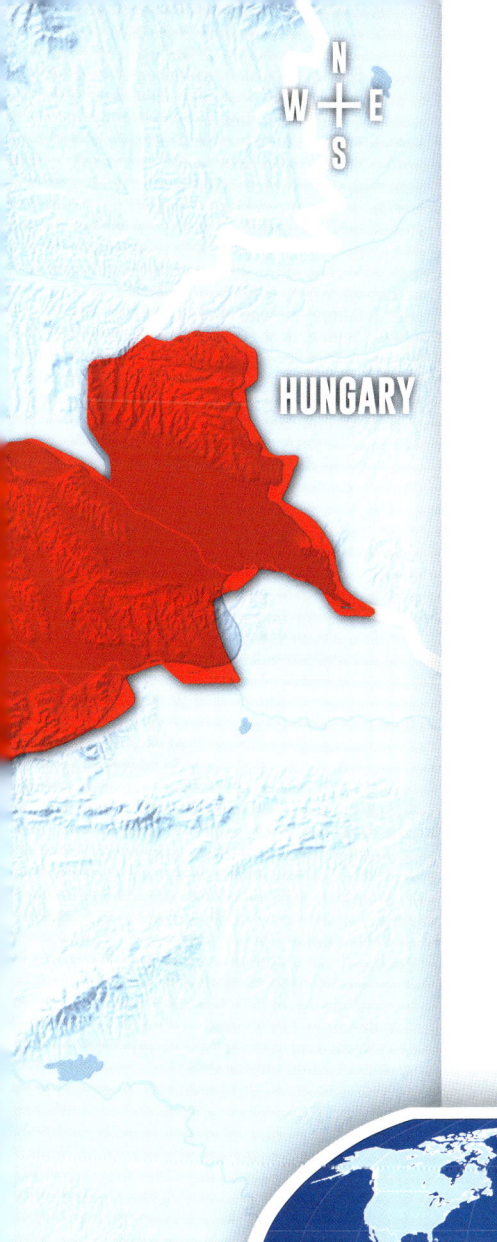

HUNGARY

Slovenia is a country in central Europe. It covers 7,827 square miles (20,273 square kilometers). In the southwest, some of Slovenia forms a small part of the Istrian **Peninsula**. This region also features the country's only coastline. It runs along the Adriatic Sea. Italy is Slovenia's western neighbor. Austria lies to the north. Hungary shares a short border to the northeast. Croatia surrounds Slovenia to the east and south.

The capital, Ljubljana, is located in the central region. It sits on the Ljubljanica River. The peaks of the Julian Alps tower over the city.

LANDSCAPE AND CLIMATE

Slovenia has a **diverse** landscape. Mountain ranges stretch from the north and northwest toward the central region. Slovenia's highest mountain, Mount Triglav, stands tall in the Julian Alps. Lake Bled and Lake Bohinj are nestled in valleys below the mountain. Limestone **plateaus** and caves stretch across the southwest. Pebble beaches run along the southwestern coastline. River valleys lie in the east and northeast.

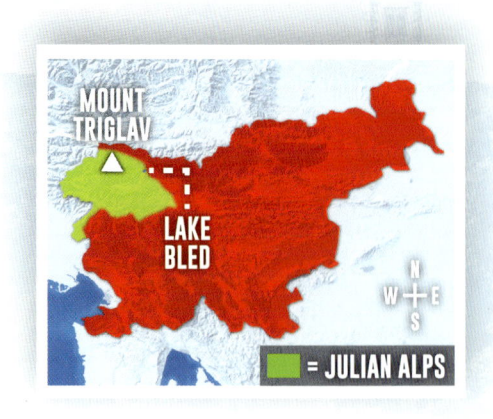

MOUNT TRIGLAV

LAKE BLED

N W E S

= JULIAN ALPS

HIDDEN ISLANDS

Slovenia has no islands along its coast. It has islands inside lakes, rivers, and even underground in caves!

LAKE BLED

MOUNT TRIGLAV

Slovenia's coast has a mild climate. Mountains are colder and snowy in winter. Rainfall usually occurs in the western and central regions in fall and spring. Most of the country has hot summers and cold winters.

Slovenia is home to many animals. Brown bears search for berries in the nation's forests. Lynxes chase after roe deer and wild boar. Ural owls peek out from tree branches. Three-toed woodpeckers and collared flycatchers fly about. Alpine ibexes **graze** on grasses along forest edges. **Native** Carniolan honeybees buzz nearby over flowering meadows. European bee-eaters fly over forests and valleys.

Grayling and trout swim in rivers while Ferruginous ducks glide over calm lakes. Blind salamanders called olms swim in watery caves. Common bottlenose dolphins swim along the coast. Red scorpionfish hunt for fish along the seafloor.

BROWN BEAR

URAL OWL

ALPINE IBEX

BEEKEEPING COUNTRY

Beekeeping is very popular in Slovenia. Carniolan bees are kept to make honey. At 1 in every 200 people, Slovenia has the most beekeepers in Europe.

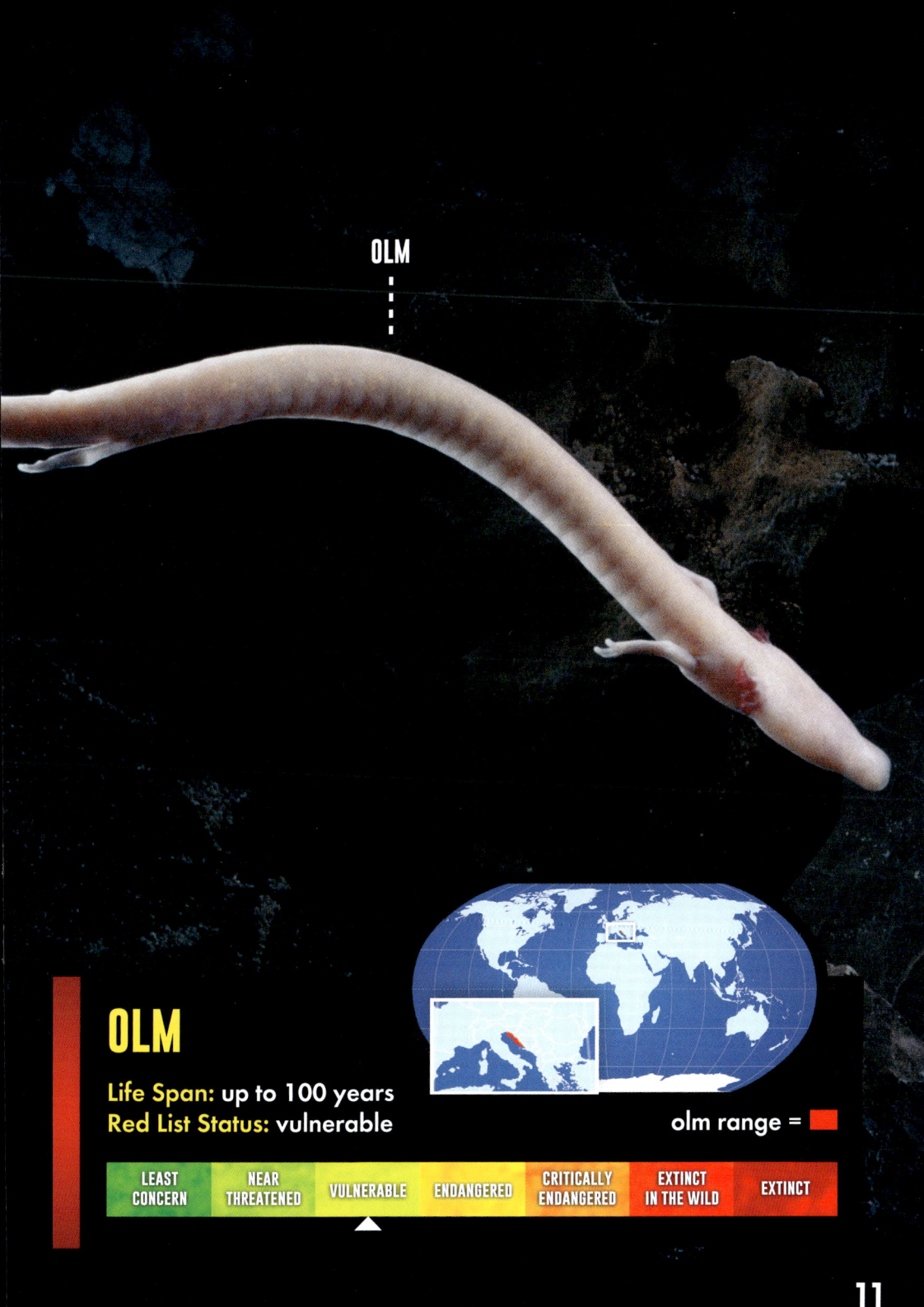

OLM

OLM

Life Span: up to 100 years
Red List Status: vulnerable

olm range =

LEAST CONCERN	NEAR THREATENED	VULNERABLE	ENDANGERED	CRITICALLY ENDANGERED	EXTINCT IN THE WILD	EXTINCT

More than 2 million people live in Slovenia. Around 8 out of 10 have a Slovene background. Other major **ethnic** groups include Serbs, Croats, and Bosniaks. More than half of all Slovenes are Catholic. Smaller numbers are another type of Christian or Muslim.

Slovene is the official language of the country. Eastern Slovenes often speak in different **dialects**. Serbian, Croatian, and Bosnian are also spoken. Hungarian and Italian are spoken near the borders of the country.

FAMOUS FACE

Name: Tina Maze
Birthday: May 2, 1983
Hometown: Črna na Koroškem, Slovenia
Famous for: A four-time Olympic medalist in Alpine skiing who has won the most medals at the Winter Olympics of any Slovene in the country's history

SPEAK SLOVENE

ENGLISH	SLOVENE	HOW TO SAY IT
hello	zdravo	ZDRAH-voh
goodbye	nasvidenje	nas-VEE-den-yuh
please	prosim	PRO-seem
thank you	hvala	huh-VAL-ah
yes	dà	DAH
no	ne	NEH

LJUBLJANA

GOING GREEN

The Green Scheme of Slovenian Tourism is a travel planning tool that supports the planet. It highlights official Green Label hotels, restaurants, and other businesses in Slovenia that pollute less.

MARIBOR

Around half of all Slovenes live in cities. Many of these **urban** dwellers call Ljubljana and Maribor home. They often live in simple concrete apartments. Some Slovenes live in towns and villages near cities. Cars are the preferred way to get around. But people also ride public trains and buses.

Houses are more common in **rural** areas. Most are modern, single-family homes. Some houses are larger. They can be home to a few generations of a family. Young Slovenes live at home until they get married or find a job. Walking and biking are popular in rural areas.

Slovenes are very polite. They greet each other with a handshake. Friends and family sometimes hug or give kisses on both cheeks. Adults address each other by title and first name.

ACCORDION

Slovenes enjoy music and dance. Many Slovenes sing in local choirs. Rural harmony singers sing soft and happy songs. They create harmonies using at least three different voices. Slovenes also dance to folk music. The polka and the waltz are popular dances. These lively tunes often feature brass and wind instruments. The native button box accordion and the zither drive the upbeat melodies.

Slovene children must attend school from ages 6 to 15. Public education is free. Students may then go to academic or **vocational** high schools. Some attend university or complete additional job training.

About three out of five Slovenes work in **service jobs**. They may work in offices, shops, or **tourism**. Some work in the medical and engineering fields. Other Slovenes work on family farms. They grow corn, wheat, and different fruit and vegetable crops. Some farms raise livestock. Slovenes also work in factories that make car parts or electrical appliances.

FARMING GRAPES

FAMOUS HORSES

The world-famous white Lipizzaner horses are originally from Lipica, Slovenia. The same farm has been breeding these horses in Lipica since 1580.

BASKETBALL

Many Slovenes enjoy playing sports. Soccer is popular year-round. Skiing is a favorite sport in winter. Basketball and hockey have become more popular over time. The national basketball and hockey teams have played in world championships.

SKIING

Slovenes also enjoy seasonal activities. Biking is popular. Some people like swimming, hiking, and running. Slovenes may spend summer vacations relaxing by the sea. Ski resorts are popular winter vacation spots. Slovenes also enjoy berry picking and mushroom hunting.

BIKING

THIEVES AND COPS

What You Need:

- a leader
- two teams with the same number of players
- an object to "steal," such as a ball

What You Do:

1. Choose one person as the leader to call out directions. Then make two teams with the same number of players. Pick a team to be the thieves and the other to be the cops.

2. Players sit in a row with their team. The thieves and cops should face each other in rows about 35 feet (11 meters) apart.

3. Give each player a number. Every thief and cop should have a number that matches a player on the other team.

4. The leader places an object in between the teams. Then they call out a player number. The thief and cop with that number walk up to the object.

5. The thief tries to distract the cop by jumping and spinning! The cop has to copy the thief.

6. The thief tries to steal the object and run back to their spot without getting caught by the cop.

7. If the cop catches the thief before the thief makes it back, the cops get a point. If the thief makes it back without getting caught, the thieves get a point.

8. The game continues until every player number has been called. The team with the most points wins. Then the teams may switch roles and start over.

FLAVOR INSPIRATIONS

Slovene cuisine has been affected by the dishes of its neighbors. Many Slovene dishes are inspired by Hungarian, Italian, and Austrian recipes.

Slovene cuisine is flavorful. Pork and beef are **staples**. Salads and roasted potatoes are common sides. For a **traditional** breakfast, Slovenes often eat bread, butter, honey, and apples. Eggs or porridge are also enjoyed. Common desserts include fruits, sweet breads, and pastries.

Lunch is the main meal. It may start with *jota*, a vegetable and bean soup. *Kranjska klobasa* may follow. These smoked sausages are served with cooked cabbage and mustard. *Ajdovi žganci*, a buckwheat porridge served with meat, is another national favorite. *Burek* is a popular street food. Its flaky dough is filled with meat and cheese.

KRANJSKA KLOBASA

BUREK

CARNIVAL FRIED DOUGH BALLS

Ingredients:
1 tablespoon yeast
2 tablespoons sugar
1/2 cup milk at room temperature
1 1/4 cups flour
4 tablespoons melted butter
3 egg yolks
salt
2 tablespoons raisins
frying oil

Steps:
1. From the measured ingredients, mix the yeast, 1 tablespoon of sugar, and 2 tablespoons of milk.

2. Put the flour in a bowl and make a hole in the middle. Pour the yeast mixture into the hole. Cover and leave it to rise for a few minutes.

3. In a separate bowl, mix the milk, melted butter, egg yolks, sugar, and a dash of salt. Combine with the yeast mixture.

4. Knead the ingredients into a soft dough. Mix in the raisins. Let it rise in a warm place for at least 1 hour, uncovered.

5. Heat up oil in a frying pan. Using a buttered spoon, gently place balls of dough in the oil and let them fry on each side until golden brown.

6. Sprinkle the dough balls with powdered sugar if desired and serve.

KURENT

Slovenes celebrate many holidays. Easter is a weeklong spring celebration. Slovenes sing, dye eggs, and attend church. Just before Lent, *Kurent* is celebrated. This Carnival event is named after a mythical figure. Many Slovenes dress up as Kurents by wearing sheepskin costumes and colorful masks. They run through town, "chasing away" winter and welcoming spring. Concerts and parades mark the celebration.

Festivals are important to Slovene culture and are held throughout the year. The Ljubljana Summer Festival draws large crowds. It is known for its music, theatre, and dance. Slovenes are happy to celebrate their rich **heritage**!

CELEBRATING THE COWS

The *Kravji Bal* is held in Bohinj every September. Locals celebrate the return of shepherds and their cattle with music after a summer of mountain grazing. The cows' milk is used to make Bohinj cheese.

TIMELINE

623 CE
King Samo establishes Slovenia and more of the Samo Empire

AROUND 2ND CENTURY BCE
Celtic people settle in what is now modern-day Slovenia

1566
The Battle of Sisak is fought between the invading Ottoman empire and the Habsburg army, stopping Ottoman expansion

AROUND 6TH CENTURY CE
Slavic settlers arrive

1282
The Habsburg Empire begins rule in Slovenia

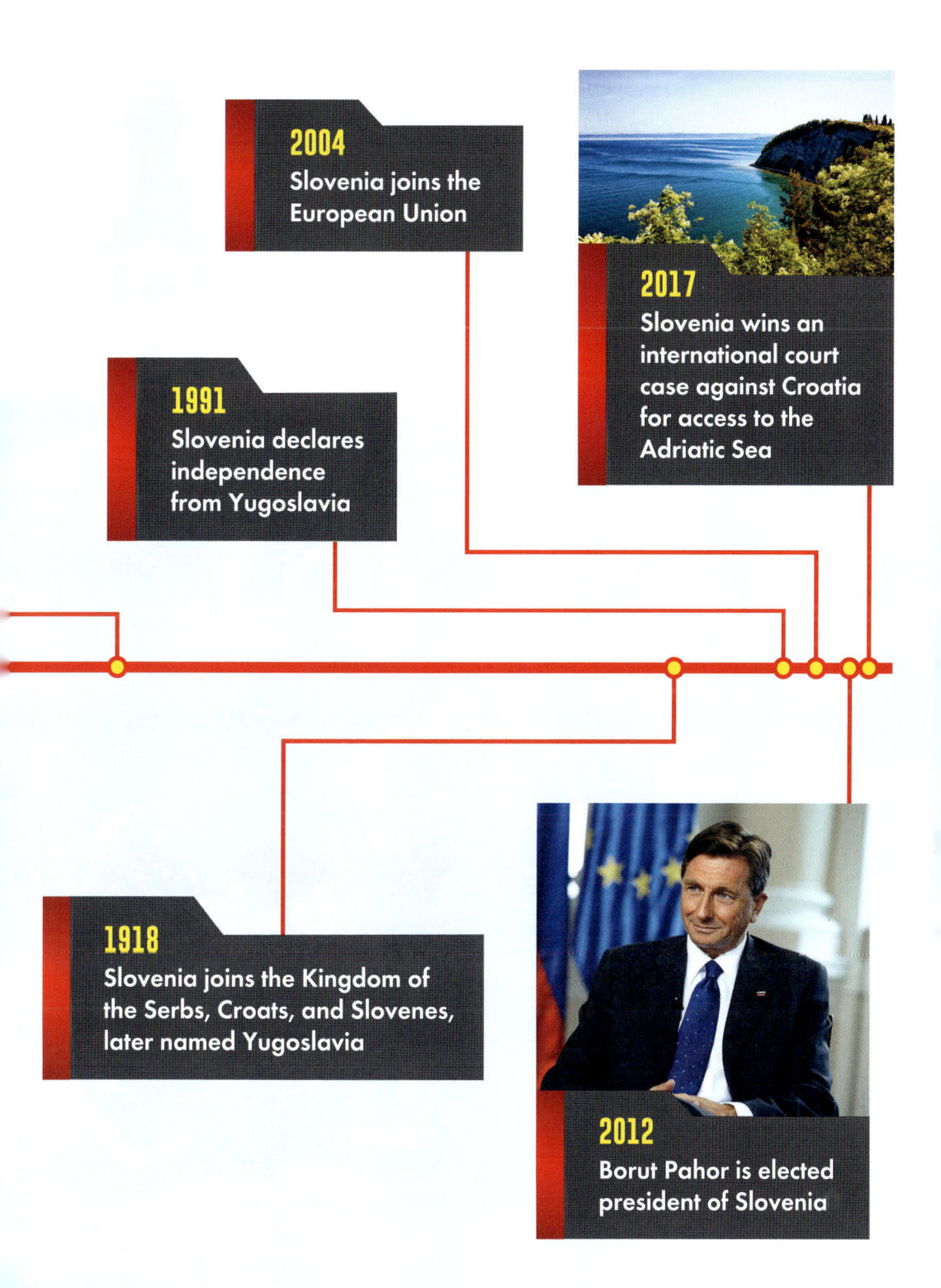

2004
Slovenia joins the European Union

2017
Slovenia wins an international court case against Croatia for access to the Adriatic Sea

1991
Slovenia declares independence from Yugoslavia

1918
Slovenia joins the Kingdom of the Serbs, Croats, and Slovenes, later named Yugoslavia

2012
Borut Pahor is elected president of Slovenia

SLOVENIA FACTS

Official Name: Republic of Slovenia

Flag of Slovenia: The Slovenian flag has three equal horizontal bands of white, blue, and red, from top to bottom. A shield in the top left corner holds the image of a white Mount Triglav. Two wavy blue lines run through the mountain. They stand for the nation's rivers and seas. Three yellow stars above the mountain represent a past Slovene dynasty.

Area: 7,827 square miles
(20,273 square kilometers)

Capital City: Ljubljana

Important Cities: Maribor, Celje, Koper

Population:
2,101,208 (2022 est.)

WHERE PEOPLE LIVE

COUNTRYSIDE
44.2%

CITY
55.8%

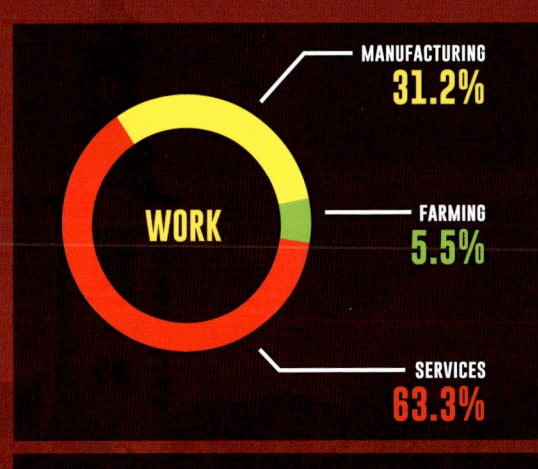

MANUFACTURING
31.2%

WORK

FARMING
5.5%

SERVICES
63.3%

Main Exports:

vehicle parts

electric machinery

medicines

wood products

National Holiday:
Statehood Day, June 25

Main Language:
Slovene (official)

Form of Government:
parliamentary republic

Title for Country Leaders:
president (chief of state), prime minister (head of government)

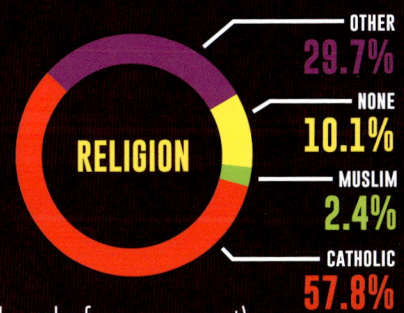

RELIGION

OTHER
29.7%

NONE
10.1%

MUSLIM
2.4%

CATHOLIC
57.8%

Unit of Money:
euro

GLOSSARY

architecture—the design of buildings and other structures

cuisine—a style of cooking

culture—the beliefs, arts, and ways of life in a place or society

dialects—local ways of speaking particular languages

diverse—made up of people or things that are different from one another

ethnic—related to a group of people who share customs and an identity

funicular—a railway that uses a cable and cars to go up and down a mountainside

graze—to eat grass or other plants that are growing in a field or pasture

heritage—the traditions, achievements, and beliefs that are part of the history of a group of people

native—originally from the area or related to things that began in the area

peninsula—a section of land that extends out from a larger piece of land and is almost completely surrounded by water

plateaus—areas of flat, raised land

rural—related to the countryside

service jobs—jobs that perform tasks for people or businesses

staples—widely used foods or other items

tourism—the business of people traveling to visit other places

traditional—related to customs, ideas, or beliefs handed down from one generation to the next

urban—related to cities and city life

vocational—involved in the training of a skill or trade that prepares an individual for a career

TO LEARN MORE

AT THE LIBRARY

Chandler, Matt. *Luka Dončić: Basketball's Breakout Star*. North Mankato, Minn.: Capstone Press, 2022.

Gottfried, Ted, and Debbie Nevins. *Slovenia*. New York, N.Y.: Cavendish Square Publishing, 2021.

Howse, Jennifer. *Croatia*. New York, N.Y.: AV2 by Weigl, 2020.

ON THE WEB

FACTSURFER

Factsurfer.com gives you a safe, fun way to find more information.

1. Go to www.factsurfer.com.

2. Enter "Slovenia" into the search box and click 🔍.

3. Select your book cover to see a list of related content.

INDEX